Living on Mars
the play

First published in 2016 by Reed Independent, Victoria, Australia.

Printed by Createspace.com, a division of Amazon.com.

Available as a printed book or an ebook from Createspace.com or Amazon.com or Kindle estores, together with most major international online outlets or bookshops with online ordering facilities:
paperback: ISBN 9780994630100
ebook: ISBN 9780994630117

Front cover: Image from Google Images. Design by Dilani Priyangika Ranaweera, Dart Lanka Productions

National Library of Australia Cataloguing-in-Publication entry:
Creator: Reed, Bill, author.
Title: Living on Mars: the play/ Bill Reed
Edition: first
ISBN: 9780994630100 (paperback)
ISBN: 9780994630117 (ebook)
Notes: includes bibliographical reference.
Subjects: Drama/black comedy
Dewey Number: A822.3

Living on Mars

The play

Bill Reed

Also by Bill Reed

Plays

Burke's Company
Bullsh/ More Bullsh
Cass Butcher Bunting
Mr Siggie Morrison with his Comb and Paper
Truganinni
Living in Black Holes (anthology)
Living on Mars (anthology)
Living on Mars: the play
Daddy the 8th
Truganinni Inside Out
Auntie and the Girl
Mirror, Mirror
Little She
You Want It, Don't You, Billy?
The Pecking Order
Jack Charles is Up and Fighting
Just Out of Your Ground
I Don't Know What to Do with You!
Paddlesteamer

novels

The Pipwink Papers\
Me, the Old Man
Stigmata
Ihe
Dogod
Crooks
Tusk
Throw her back
Are You Human?
Tasker Tusker Tasker
Awash
1001 Lankan Nights book 1
1001 Lankan Nights book 2
Passing Strange

Nonfiction

Water Workout

Award-winning short stories (see also title 'Passing Strange')

Messman on the C.E. Altar
The 200-year Old Feet
The Case Inside
Blind Freddie Among the Pickle Jars
The Old Ex-serviceman
The Shades of You my Dandenong

The earlier version of this play had the alternative titles of 'Familiar Parts' and 'The Klutz Holding the Pickle Jars'. It was short listed for MTC season of 2007 and 'long listed' for the season 2008 respectively.

It is the title play in the anthology 'Living on Mars' published in 2015 under the ISBNs 9780994322784 (paperback) and 9780994322791 (ebook).

It has also gained selection to be listed on the Australian Script Centre's website Australianplays.org.

The Setting

The play is set in a well-to-do house in Port Moresby.

Directing note:
Henry Gasser is blind. The first half of the play can be presented with him closeted in his own light and the actors coming into his 'sphere'. Or the actors can address themselves to the audience under spotlight as though the audience is Henry Gasser -- that is, there is the element of whether this is only happening in Henry's mind.

The second half is presented in full stage lighting, but with an umbra centred on Henry.

Character note:
Henry should be played as though he was a blind comedian, such that his cynicism does not seem overarchingly bitter and, therefore, unsustainable.

The Characters

HENRY GASSER
An expat Australian. If he is remembered at all, it is as the son of Professor William E, L. J. Gasser -- the 'pioneering' anthropologist in the field of the Australian Aborigines – and, in consequence, as the keeper of his father's infamous Aboriginal 'parts' collection which he obstinately refuses to give back to the nation.

CLARISSA GASSER
Henry's younger wife. Of Tamil local-PNG stock, ending her forties, but handsome still. Her years of poverty won't stop itching her… and she doesn't want it to.

GARY
Mid-thirties. Australian. Mature PhD student let loose from Sydney Uni. Making the most of his semester break. The peculiar watch-and-wait quality of a kinder heart than appearance.

MARGARET
Clarissa's 'local' cousin, and man-eater of the species whenever employed in well-to-do households. 'Sir, that man beat me.' and her bruises are a known money-spinning asset of hers. Sex is the hand out for the hand-outs.

KEKE
Margaret's 'local' husband. Melanesian. Sinewy and sinister as his pride of place of being a real rogue requires. Sarong, bare feet, and no looking sideways at him... nothing personal; he'll just gut you.

Act 1

(Henry sits in his cocoon of light. Around him is a darkness which at times will seem to throb with presences. These could be the other actors, or shadows that he senses from time to time that make him stop expectantly, fearfully.

Over the outside sounds of the mosques and temples, sound grows of a morning BBC sports report. Henry finally turns it off. He is sitting in a commode chair next to a night table. When the wrong alarm setting has the radio turn back on again suddenly, he reached out too hard to turn it off again, he only succeeds in knocking a plate to the floor.

This flusters him. He manages to pick the plate up, but then gropes around unsuccessfully for the morning banana that should have been on it. It wasn't.

The phone, on a charging cradle at his side, rings. He reaches up for it, automatically switches it to speaker. Before he speaks:)

VOICE: Don't let them see you on your knees, Henry.

HENRY: Who's this?

VOICE: Who do you think it is? Anyway, there's no banana today. It's seeing as how today's not your usual day, you know that.

HENRY: (calls) PREMA…?

VOICE: No Prema, either. No housekeeper this day, Henry. Just her little gesture of leaving your morning banana a little to the left. No, to your right. No, your left. Did you notice? Oops, of course you couldn't. Aw, shame.

HENRY: (calls again) PREMA!

VOICE: You forgot to ask who I am a second time.

HENRY: Fuck who you are. Who cares about grovelling? You don't tell me about grovelling. Back in the days when seeing was all the rage, mate, I was the world's best groveller. When I grovelled the world pointed, but I've retired from the grovel, so up yours.

(*he listens for a reply, but phone has gone silent*)

That's right. Sod off.

(*then calls out yet again*)

PREMA? CLARISSA?

(*no response but suddenly 'feels' movement around*)

Who're you?!

(*gropes aggressively and causes the plate to fall again*)

Goddamn it!

(*struggles to gather himself, then knocks the phone off*)

Shit. On. It.

(*gets to his knees again, gropes now for phone*)

MY PEE AND YOUR LEG, PREMA AND BLOODY CLARISSA!

(*finally 'asks' the darkness*)

Is that you there, Clarissa?

(The phone rings again. He answers it keenly, listens warily before talking, but only gets someone whistling brightly. This is actually frightening.

He replaces the phone, then feels the dark spaces around him 'shift' once more)

HENRY: (gives in to pathos) Oh, Christ.

(*then, but out of fear*)

CLARISSA? YOU THINK YOU'VE GOT TITS BUT THEY'RE PAINT JOBS!

(*and to the shadows around*)

Bury me down old Mexico way, why don't you? 'Here lies Henry Gasser, fuctus cactus.'

(the phone voice suddenly starts up again. Again he obliges by picking it up)

VOICE: Now you're just being maudlin, Henry.

HENRY: It's not being bloody maudlin. It's being shitty-livered. It's the bloody BBC. I hate the BBC. All it does it talk about skinny little sods running around trying to kick the bejesus out of a round pig's bowel. You show me a pig that's got a round bowel. Maybe they have, but why should the whole of Planet Earth stay tuned? Anyway, you piss off. If you want to speak to my wife Clarissa, piss off anyway.

(VOICE makes a sudden aggressive scream, succeeds in being frightening again. HENRY 'feels' it as another alarming movement around.)

HENRY: Who's there?
(*swings his arms in real defense until he stops and sniffs*)
Who whacked in?

VOICE: (turns sadistic) See, it's this brilliant sunny day outside, Henry. Pity you can't see it, Henry, or you'd see why Clarissa is seriously debunking the coop.

(the phone goes dead. HENRY waits until he is sure it has, replaces receiver. Then speaks to 'dead' phone:)

HENRY: I don't believe in ghosts, you dork.

(Suddenly, unexpectedly 'appearing' in his spotlight:)

CLARISSA: You don't think?

HENRY: Clarissa!

CLARISSA: Clarissa what?

HENRY: (mimic) 'Clarissa what?' Is that all you've got to say, bloody Clarissa?

(*no answer*)

I tell you what, Clarissa. I should be complaining but I am not complaining.... like a little care and attention and things. Bananas!

CLARISSA: (dully) Bananas.

HENRY: Bloody bananas, bloody Clarissa! But what're you going on about bananas for? What I'm complaining about is you going at all that slurping in the middle of the night. It's downright rude. Frankly it sounds terrible even as an onomatopoeia.

CLARISSA: Oh, I don't know about that. It felt quite nice.

HENRY: No way; not the way you slurp.

(he spins around too fast to follow her movement, nearly knocks the light over.)

CLARISSA: Careful!

HENRY: (outcry) Who are you slurping with out there?

CLARISSA: My business.

HENRY: Any slurp in this house in the middle of the night is my business. I'm trying to get some shuteye here, bloody Clarissa.

CLARISSA: Well, you won't have to put up with it much longer, Henry.

HENRY: About time

CLARISSA: And I don't slurp.

HENRY: You say that about snoring. At least with snoring you're slurping alone.

CLARISSA: Just so you don't say I didn't give you fair warning, Henry.

HENRY: (sniffing) That's that perfume I bought you.

CLARISSA: I'm not wearing any perfume, Henry.

HENRY: (furious with the logic) I had to search the perfume haunts of the world to find one strong enough to overcome your body-odour, Clarissa. A bit of appreciation might help.

CLARISSA: (shadow withdrawing) Oh well, if you're going to go like that again…

(She has moved well into the darker areas.

Just as suddenly as it went off, the radio comes back on, but this time with much more volume than before. He leaves the BBC sports report on, shouts over)

HENRY: That's not funny, Clarissa!

(The radio turns off again. There is a silence)

HENRY: You there?

CLARISSA: (re-appearing) You've got your silly morning banana.

HENRY: No, I haven't! Look, it fell on the floor. It crashed into awful little pieces at my feet and that makes it a tragic thing when it comes to the ritual of the morning banana!

CLARISSA: See, what I think is you shifted position. Have you shifted your bum, Henry?

HENRY: Is that an attempt at humour?

CLARISSA: I think you shifted your bum out of arm's reach and just because your arm's now too short to reach your precious banana, you're trying to blame Prema and us.

HENRY: 'Us' bloody who?

(Around, there seems to be an answering guffaw)

HENRY: I heard that. You tell that *slurper* to get out of my house, bloody Clarissa!

CLARISSA: Please don't start that slurping nonsense again. You might think it's funny. I don't think so.

HENRY: Your witching-hour caterwauls, Clarissa.

(She actually giggles, but it comes over doubled with someone else's giggle)

HENRY: (sotto voce, with ear cocked) If you must know, I always thought your caterwauls were more like honks than a caterwauls, Clarissa. I keep saying passion is not breaking wind, Clarissa, but you refuse to listen. If you're going to slurp, slurp properly.
(*into other space at maybe other person*)
You hear that, Slurp old fruit…?

CLARISSA: Just who are you talking to, Henry?

HENRY: (waves that off) Anyway, what're you doing here, Clarissa?

CLARISSA: You might remember you called.

HENRY: I was calling Prema, nosey.

CLARISSA: Prema went off.

HENRY: Went off?

CLARISSA: Went off.

HENRY: She started growing mold, Clarissa?

CLARISSA: That's right; out come the sarcastics. She went off you, Henry. What you did made her sick to her stomach. And she's only the housekeeper.

HENRY: (stubbornly) I did nothing to be ashamed of.

CLARISSA: That lady will never believe in the goodness of human nature again.

HENRY: (sudden remorse) I was underage!

CLARISSA: You? Bite this. Prema told me all your victims were underage.

HENRY: (guilt-ridden) They all looked like in their forties or fifties to me. How was I to know they were underage? I just looked up. I thought they said bait knife not gaol bait. If I hadn't slipped in that pool of blood in my flippers, it would have…

(She withdraws into the surrounding shadows.

He senses she has gone, has a panic attack, fights for breath

.

She re-emerges into his light to steady him; rubs his back, shushes him until he calms down and can sit back again.)

HENRY: (momentarily spent) I don't deserve that… slurping noise. You get that cut right out, Clarissa.

CLARISSA: Sympathy isn't going to keep me here this time. Sorry.

HENRY: Take my father's books with you!

CLARISSA: No way.

HENRY: It's his fortieth tomorrow, or whatever when! They'd have thought up some new bloody medal thing to honour him just to dishonour me! If you don't take his books, how can I admit I've never read a word of any of them? I'm sick of sounding like the ingrate!

CLARISSA: You've gotten sick of everyone and everything, Henry. You any idea how ordinary that makes you sound?

HENRY: More than being married to you, bloody Clarissa?

CLARISSA: Your father was a great man.

(He groans, but is relieved of this when the phone rings again. He is quick to it this time)

VOICE: D'you think that's fair, Henry? A tonne of books in the mini-cab that's on its way out here right now in this brilliant sunshine, where all others can see clearly now?   Where would she sit? Where would anyone with her sit? Her lap as you know is as wide as the Indian Ocean, even if it is full of sharks, ha ha. You see the problem?

HENRY: (desperately) You're wanted on the phone, Clarissa.

(She emerges to take up the receiver, hears nothing, jams it back on its cradle with disgust. Moves back into shadows as:)

HENRY: (sniffs the air)   Perfume. I told you. Ambergris or, if I remember, humpback piss. I got this discount because they said it dripped out of the bruised end of a dying whale. When I said that sounded just right for my wife, they gave it on discount; when they heard you were my wife, they doubled it. Nice glad-to-be-alive day out, is it, or just trying to cover up your athlete's foot?

CLARISSA: (giggle) Silly.

(Now he seems to definitely hear a chortle of some shared joke)

HENRY: Who're you saying 'silly' to?

CLARISSA: Wouldn't you like to know.

HENRY: I heard that attempt at a daytime slurp, Clarissa!

CLARISSA: (receding) Silly.

HENRY: Up yours with silly, Clarissa! Don't think I can't smell testosterone when it's on the nose.
(*calls out 'past' her*)
Hey, yo, Slurp old son, I get it. Blind Man's Bluff your thing, is it? Hoick her and honk me, right?

(The phone rings again. He knocks it to the floor trying to answer it, but that lifts the receiver anyway...)

VOICE: Don't be like that, Hen.

HENRY: (outcry) Clarissa, tell him he's too near!

CLARISSA: (shadowy but nearer) Henry, you'd hear footsteps if you were drowning.

(The sound of her voice settles him down. He manages to rescue the phone and can speak back to it with equanimity)

HENRY: I don't know who you are, Slurp old sausage, but you're obviously in cahoots with my wife. I don't know what cahoots with Clarissa actually means, but I do know you should quicksmart apply for a Red Crescent needle just in case. Save yourself before Clarissa blots out your sun. Oh, I have known how the padded cell can come before the hospital cot! This is insight I'm giving you now. Call me blind old Tiresias or I won't see you again, ha ha.

(he waits, but nothing out of phone)

Oh, sure, you can go all dumbie now, Slurp you dumbie. You are already feeling how it mightn't be just a fork in the road but actually full-on Clarissa. I'm telling you that is precisely what Arabia thinks of America and Arabia's on the side of scorpions; shows you how bad. So what if Henry can't lift blocks of concrete on the strength of his penis anymore? Well, at least, not higher than a cherry picker on stilts. Slurpings ain't everything.

(He only shrugs when he gets nothing back out of the phone, but is sombre again when CLARISSA returns to his sphere of light)

CLARISSA: Henry?

HENRY: Let in some light, Clarissa.

CLARISSA: There is plenty of light.

HENRY: Clarissa, let in some air.

CLARISSA: There's plenty of air.

HENRY: Clarissa, let in some breathing room.

CLARISSA: That's what I'm out to do, Henry.

(She leaves the light; he listens hard for a moment)

HENRY: (back to the phone) It's the slippery skin of the thing, you see, old pie-and-peas. It's all connected with morning bananas and whether they do or don't make you regular.

VOICE: (suddenly) Go on with you…

HENRY: (brightening) Go on what?

VOICE: It's not the morning bananas. It's the slippery slope between the eyes, isn't it?

HENRY: Blood oath! If I had eyes, I'd be homing my steel caps at Clarissa's quoit.

(*irrelevant*)

You know they called it a bait knife and I was thinking when it somehow came up from the muddy depths that it hurt, it hurt…

(*stops, gathers himself to whisper*)

Listen, I get the slurps loud and clear but how much do you think she really hears any of this?

CLARISSA: (from 'around') I hear plenty. As loudly as your brain rattles, Henry Gusser!

HENRY: Gasser, you dummy! Jesus H, Clarissa, six years of marriage...

(*then happily back to phone*)

True, that, old fruit, she's dead right. Let's say her sloppy Mr Slurp had the gall to come downstairs with her. Let's say they called him a nice sharp bait knife too. He would be confronted by my dicey ticker, as eyeless in Gasser as it would be in Gaza or even gaze. I also have a bit of a dicey heart, he should keep the frights down a bit, all right? You may chuckle, if that's your beer, but the main thing is he should not trip up or over the specimen jars, or he'd be confronted by the ghosts of Aboriginal Australia and nobody would wish that on anyone, not on my watch.

(*then 'out' to CLARISSA*)

Clarissa, take the fucking books, but keep his mitts off the pickle jars.

(*back to phone*)

All this is called wedded bliss.

VOICE: I can see that clearly.

HENRY: (stopping) How?

VOICE: Figuratively speaking, Henry. Though it's not a bad figure at all, either.

HENRY: Ah, yes, Clarissa the dish. Clarissa Issa Looker. Light and creamy is she. Succulent as any Indian mix should be. Eurasian cross to you, old suck-it-and-see Oft, I call her Big Mac, as in you have to go past the greasy mouthful. Poor she was, but sumptuous at pretending. Straight off, we recognised our mutual penchant for outrageous lies.

(With a dismissive grunt, she comes back into view)

CLARISSA: (not too unkindly) And then you went blind.

(HENRY stops, shocked)

VOICE: And you were wondering if she might have been listening.

HENRY: (at 'it') Go fart in your futon!

(and slams off phone, returns to where he thinks CLARISSA is)

HENRY: 'And then you went blind'. Oh, sure, Clarissa, I deliberately went blind to spite you. What is this: an attempt at brutal honesty? CLARISSA, TO YOU SOMETHING BRUTALLY HONEST IS AN ITCH BELOW THE NAVEL.
(*as a sudden thought*)
Jesus H., Clarissa, don't tell me old Slurp's another one of your third cousins or something!

CLARISSA: And I've told you not to talk about my family like that.

HENRY: That's all right for you, Clarissa! I could handle the five brothers you trotted out at the engagement, but not the scrum of unmarried sisters who were attacking the wedding gifts with their twenty-five sons and forty-five daughters and counting. It's not a crime to keep their legs closed, you know.

CLARISSA: (withdrawing again) You're disgusting and I'm going.

HENRY: Don't go!

CLARISSA: I'm going.

HENRY: (panicky) Jesus H... where's Prema?!

CLARISSA: You keep asking that after what she saw?

HENRY: (outcry) She didn't see anything!

CLARISSA: She saw enough to make her want to puke, that's all
(*gets annoyed at his fumbling*)
Henry, there is no thermos.

HENRY: (defiant) Isn't there.

CLARISSA: No.

HENRY: Bloody is.

CLARISSA: Bloody isn't!

(But he finds it under table and brandishes it)

CLARISSA: Give me that thing!

(They have a childish tug-of-was over a thermos flask. She wins)

CLARISSA: Honestly, you're a child, Henry Gasser.
(*then sweetly*)
Would you like tea too?

HENRY: Who're you asking?

CLARISSA: (fading into shadows) I've already said you wish it was so easy.

HENRY: What's that mean?!
(*but he rightfully senses she has left. He calls after her*)
Oh, yeah, Clarissa, and smart move to tell you're leaving me to your family. With their teeth, the walls of this house are only made of bricks and mortar, you know. Jesus H., Clarissa, don't leave me with more of you!
(*listens, but nothing*)
Clarissa?
(*calls*)
COME BACK, CLARISSA, I MISS YOUR BALD BITS ALREADY!

(and gets a belly laugh in before solitude closes in again. The phone rings again. This time he is eager for it)

VOICE: I can see your mind's eye, Hen. It's a worrying time, I know. Prema couldn't bring the banana because this morning the banana guy's wife's lover strangled him with his own bicycle chain and Prema's not shouting at the gardener from the kitchen because she's missing in action and he's sitting around clipping his toenails. School kids haven't annoyed the living Christ out of you by ringing the gate bell. You're feeling left out of things. You feel you could yodel and not hit anyone with a breath that's lost its touch with Pepsodent. Hen. If you had someone to turn up the overhead fan you might be able to flush out the vacuum. But… well, you see what's wrong with that, don't you?

HENRY: The shag what?

VOICE: You don't know who's paying for this phone call, ha ha.

HENRY: Bugger!
(*hiss at phone*)
You got any idea?

VOICE: How would I? I'm a phone.

HENRY: Smart arse!

(He slams down phone, then suddenly decides to take a series of deep breaths.

All around is instant and echoing breathing too, taken in unison in the surrounding darkness – until he suddenly stops to listen again. It stops. He starts again. It starts again. He stops; it stops.

As an exercise in trying to discover if someone is there, it proves nothing conclusive)

HENRY: (to 'around') Clever, old franger. Clarissa trained you up on Henry's little tricks, has she? Vee impressive, actually. Bit of a heavy-breather of a deep-sea snorkler myself once, too before I got between the bait knife and the surface. But enough of pleasantries…
(*calls*)
CLARISSA?

CLARISSA: (further off) Coming. Either that or it's a meltdown, whoo-ee!

HENRY: (out to her) You've always lacked class, Clarissa.

CLARISSA: Yeah, and I lack it more now.

(Yet again, he is positive he hears a chuckling response to her nearby. He struggles to alleviate that anxiety)

HENRY: You tell that slurper of yours they didn't call me the Vladimir Vladimirovich Nabokov of the South Seas for nothing, Clarissa. Somebody who will remain infallible forever once said if I was more Nabokov you'd be Lolita. I don't know about that, but you couldn't be more Lolita.

(*to other dark area*)
Nabokov, old Slurp, old son. Oi, you ever see the film they made of his 'Laughter in the Dark', old franger? Where you and her go slurp slurp slurp hammer-and-tongs all night long and just out of the old man's reach, giggle giggle, bait, bait? No?
(*silence*)
Yes?
(*silence. Then in blind panic*)
I'm not a brave man!

(He fights to regain composure, but is really trying playing doggo. Stops his breathing yet again in another attempt to catch a sound of the other man.)

HENRY: (unconvincingly) I heard that!
(*the phone rings again. He snatches it up, into it*:)
You hear that too?

VOICE: Nope.

HENRY: Then what're you calling for?

VOICE: Just to tell you you didn't hear it.

(HENRY slams the receiver down in disgust

HENRY: (to the darkness around) Ok, I've done my share of funking out in my day too. You watch out yourself, Slurp, you sod, because it was Clarissa who led me into the worst funk of my life. She bloodywell convinced me to use the local eye surgeon because he needed the step up to Rich World experience. She didn't say the only step up the bugger needed was the last payment on his sixty-foot yacht? And when I said what're you done to my last eye, you prick?, you know what he said? He said, 'Go back home, Mr Gasser; you're lost your sense of humour'.
(*hard chuckle*)
Cheeky bugger gives my eye the barbeque fork, then kills me with logic.
(*suddenly maudlin again*)

Give me your hand, Clarissa Issa.

CLARISSA: (in shadows, but giving it) Now you're being silly.

HENRY: It's a smooth hand, Issa. Buttery. A most wonderful creamiment. A beautiful woman's hand still.
(*keeps hold but talks past her*)
Old Slurp of the sleepless nights, you noticed how the subcontinental women are lusty and busty and forthright thrusty and built like the goddess with all those hunky hocks to high heaven? They are their men's torment, those lovely bums.
(*then*)
Don't pull away, Issa. I only want both hands.

CLARISSA: (giggling with the other arm being held in shadow) Well, you can't have both hands.

HENRY: Why?

CLARISSA: (sickly inferring) Don't tell me you can't guess.

HENRY: (angrily) Give me your other hand, bloody Clarissa!

CLARISSA: Ow!

(She struggles against being pulled in two directions. Henry feels this and gets, of course, the confirmation he has been waiting for.

He loses the tug-of-war but manages to keep hold of her arm, then stops, stunned with the realisation...)

HENRY: (hiss) He's right here!

CLARISSA: (now stretched out Christ-like) Who is?

HENRY: (deadly serious) Clarissa, promise you won't leave me alone with my thoughts!

CLARISSA: (avoiding emotional trap) For God's sake, Henry, what's wrong with you this morning?

HENRY: Oh, only that we're never going to see each other again. How's that for a start?

CLARISSA: You know how weird 'see' in that context sounds?

HENRY: (petulant) So what?
(*then*)
By the way, if not family, local buck off the street is he?

CLARISSA: Now you're getting really unpleasant.

HENRY: (mimic) ' Now you're getting really unpleasant '
(*then*)
Clarissa, don't do this. All I did was go and get a bit blind-sided, that's all.

CLARISSA: (surprising sadness) Henry, you never got blindsided in your life.

HENRY: (given hope) Ah, my Clarissa-Issa. I gave you no Taj Mahal, did I? But you, you see, you never ever could be the real Queen Mumtaz or me your Shah. And, I know, I know, all you wanted was to have us photographed kissing cheeks in front of the place.
(*quickly*)
Look, if I told you were right…?

CLARISSA: Don't start now.

HENRY: I know, I know, I stopped looking at you.

CLARISSA: Ha.

HENRY: No, really. How many of our six years would you allow as good?

CLARISSA: I'd say five.

HENRY: That's not half bad!

CLARISSA: Five weeks.

HENRY: No, no, no, Clarissa.

CLARISSA: No, no, no, what?

HENRY: If you think I'm going to believe I've travelled the world only to have my jugular ripped out by some all-muscle-and-bone slurper off a local corner… okay I'll buy that. But, if he's pasty-faced whitie with tattoos he reckons are better than our Highlands… I'm saying no going getting all crass on me, Clarissa. That's what I'm saying.

CLARISSA: (quite cheerfully) Here's a point… how could a perfect crime be crass?

HENRY: (stopping, wary) What crime?

CLARISSA: (gaily) Oh, I couldn't tell you that. It wouldn't be perfect if I did.

HENRY: I'm not having something perfect perpetuated on me, Clarissa!

CLARISSA: Why not? I'd think you'd think it would be a nice touch.

HENRY: I'll tell you why not, bloody Clarissa. Because it would look all old-colonial and gin-and-tonic messy! You know very well messy does not run in the Gasser family, Clarissa. My father used to drain messies into gutters running along the sides of his dissecting table and all the cockroaches had to do was wait patiently outside by the open drain by his order. That's how you treat messies, Clarissa. Outside. Anyway, you cut this out, Clarissa. Crass is crass.

CLARISSA: (chortles ‘out’ to shadows) Did you see that? That might look like a pout, but it’s when he’s trying to look outraged.

HENRY: (absolutely indignant) Are you conceivably talking about me?

CLARISSA: And that, that going all indignant thing he's trying now? That's always just made his eyes pop. I call it his cod’s eye look.

HENRY: Jesus H., Clarissa!

(In his agitation, he grabs up the phone and appeals to it)

HENRY: You just going to sit there?

VOICE: Leave me out of it.

.

(HENRY thrusts the receiver down, misses and the phone falls to the floor again, despite his attempts to catch it)

HENRY: (whine) Leave it for Prema to pick up.

CLARISSA: I told you, Prema's not setting a foot in this house again.

HENRY: (sudden guilt again) It wasn’t like it seemed!

CLARISSA: Wasn’t it.

HENRY: No, it wasn’t. They laughed and said 'shove it right in'!

CLARISSA: They were all underage but who’s trying to depress you anyway, Henry?

HENRY: (whinishly) Maybe a little soothing, Clarissa.

CLARISSA: Hold on a minute.

(She goes from his presence for an alarming time and whispers off in the shadows. When she returns:)

CLARISSA: Henry, it seems it's time to go.

HENRY: (self-righteous survival instinct) Stuff it, Clarissa, you're not allowed to swank in and out like it's some cheap slurp hotel.

CLARISSA: (cheerily) What's wrong cheap slurp hotels?

HENRY: Wrong?! Because I'm frothing here, Clarissa! This is blindness you're dealing with. This is me being scared witless blind, Clarissa. I want to scream every minute away. I want to screech fright at even the thought of falling asleep. I've got such self-pity in here that I can't even enjoy it. No, it's even worse than blindness. This is Colonel-Blimp blindness. This is being ridiculous and blind.

(There is an appropriate silence, and then, somewhat shockingly, a loud raspberry from deep in the shadows)

HENRY: How dare you! What a dog of a thing, Clarissa.

CLARISSA: (from far away) It wasn't me.

HENRY: Crap, Clarissa.

CLARISSA: (fading) Henry, it really is getting late.

HENRY: All right, then, Clarissa, as I see it you're down to two options. Number one is just stay and I regret that for the rest of my life, ha ha.
(*listens*)
You there?

CLARISSA: (but muffled as though mouth full) Mmmm?

HENRY: Please pay attention while your limited span lasts, Clarissa. Option two is once a week or so, with my permission, you glue the saggy bits down and scoot along to the pool and indulge that penchant for the local lads that you local tawdry older women have.

(Long pause, before:)

CLARISSA: (mouth still full) I don't know whether I can go through with this today.

HENRY: That's not to me!
(*hopeful hiss*)
Clarissa? Did he answer?

(She re-appears in his light)

CLARISSA: (throwing back logic) Didn't you just say 'he' couldn't exist?

HENRY: Hey, I'm blind in here, Clarissa.

CLARISSA: Sorry, Henry, but he's right. If we put it off today, we'll put it off tomorrow. And he's trying to break me of being a habit person.
(*chattily*)
I feel a better person for it already.

HENRY: (real fear again) Forget 'it'! He doesn't mean 'it'!

CLARISSA: I'm afraid he does.

HENRY: What does he want to do?

CLARISSA: I wish I knew!

(There is now a shocked pause)

CLARISSA: (a moment's awareness) Both of you... I think I'm really going to have to stop all this.

HENRY: (grasps opportunity) You shouldn't be made to undergo queasiness, Clarissa, not with the way you put on make-up. You know what I think? I think there's a feminine streak in all this, isn't there?

CLARISSA: You're not making things any easier, Henry.

HENRY: It's you and Prema! The Gasser homies together on the slippery slurp! That's upchuckable, Clarissa. No, I take that back. It's quite nice on the metaphor scale, that. Ms Slurp's better than Mr Slurp or even Master Slurp, knowing you.

(*calls*)

PREMA, IT'S ONLY YOUR BEARD NOT A BODY-SHOP PIPE CLEANER!

(*no answer of course, but still 'around' to Prema*)

I didn't think you had it in you, Prema, with your chassis swung so low. Just that, before you slit my throat in a lover's rage, Prema, any chance of a last brew? Oh, and were you told I didn't see the morning's banana?

CLARISSA: Henry, just shut up! It is not Prema.

HENRY: (suddenly weary) Look, you dill, just tell him to get on with it.

CLARISSA: (ditto) He doesn't want to yet. He's upset about how you can dismiss him so easily when you can't even see him. He has a point, you know.

HENRY: (thus sees a con) Proof of him, Clarissa, right now! Give your hands!

CLARISSA: Let's not go through that again.

HENRY: Both hands!

CLARISSA: What do you think might have changed, Henry?

HENRY: I don't believe there's any Slurp sod at all out there, Clarissa.

CLARISSA: (to other side of her) He wants to know if you'll relinquish that hand.

HENRY: (near fury) I want that other hand!

CLARISSA: This one?

HENRY: And the other one, bloody Clarissa.

CLARISSA: You've got both hands, Henry.

HENRY: (dumb pause, before) If I concede that, don't think I'm admitting anything.

CLARISSA: (waiting) So?

HENRY: (suspiciously) So, what's he holding then?

CLARISSA: Of me? Well, let's say I'd like one hand back so I can show him what I mean about ooo down a bit...

HENRY: (tight-lipped) Clarissa, I'm going to rap both your knuckles on the table and I'm going to keep holding your dukes and old Slurp vegemite out there has to do some knocking back since you can't. All right? You ready?

CLARISSA: He nods why not if it amuses you.

(He knocks her knuckles on the table, listens. But no response.)

HENRY: (triumphantly) There! So knacker off that nonsense about some other human being might be so desperate as to come at you, Clarissa.

CLARISSA: You can insult away but he wasn't ready.

HENRY: Rubbish.

(Then comes a very belated knocking 'answer'. HENRY quickly tries to grab her hands back but is too late.)

HENRY: Ha bloody ha, Clarissa.

CLARISSA: I think he's got the hang of it now, Henry.
(*grabbing his hands this time*)
Let's try again.

(She raps her knuckles – her hands in his hands -- on the table. This time there is an immediate response. In fun, she does it again. The echoing response is not only more lively, but takes up a beat.)

HENRY: (pulling hands away) How are you doing that?

CLARISSA: It's only Gary, silly.

GARY: (out of shadows) Gah-rry, that's me.

HENRY: (real fear now) Oh God!

CLARISSA: (to the 'GARY' shadow area) Getting on, he's gets turns.

GARY: Knock, knock, who's turn?

(She giggles, moves compliantly into the shadows. They obviously engage in some sexual foreplay just outside HENRY's light).

HENRY: (just managing it) YOU CUT THAT OUT, CLARISSA!

GARY: Hey, anyone hear Nabokov of the Arctic Ocean…?

HENRY: (fury to the rescue) The South Seas, you ignoramus! I object to this ignoramus slurping around my house, bloody Clarissa, but what I object to more is him not listening when his betters are talking.
(*calls*)
PREMA, WHERE ARE YOU?

CLARISSA: (re his shouting) Shit! Don't keep doing that, Henry.

(She notices – and we can just discern – GARY using his mobile phone to dial HENRY's number. HENRY grabs his ringing phone as a lifeline)

HENRY: (into receiver) Call the police!

GARY = VOICE: Henry?

HENRY: *Where did you go?*

GARY = VOICE: Me? How? I'm just a ring, Hen.

(But only just gets that out after CLARISSA understands what GARY has been doing and wrestles with him to try to take the mobile phone.)

HENRY: Hello…? Hello…?

CLARISSA: (furious to GARY) No more humiliation.

GARY: (but giving in) He's into it now.

HENRY: (into phone) Into what?
(*then into air*)
Into what?

(There is a silence – awkward between CLARISSA and

GARY as they fade again; perplexed for HENRY.

Finally, HENRY listens one last time into the phone, gives it up with)

HENRY: (weak bravado) You tell that Slurp s'head to watch it.

(There are sounds of glass butting up against glass. The shock snaps him out of himself)

HENRY: Clarissa, keep him away from the jars!

(He is alone again.

Long listening pause before slurping sounds again)

HENRY: Jesus H., Clarissa!

(She returns straightening her dress. He senses her presence finally.)

HENRY: Clarissa, kindly tell that slurping maniac there's half of the Pitjantjarajara tribe in those jars. The famous half.

CLARISSA: (overshoulder) It's his Daddy's precious body parts.

HENRY: I won't have you saying 'body parts' all snooty like that, bloody Clarissa. They are huntings and they are gatherings.

CLARISSA: In Australia, they keep screaming for him to return them to their rightful owners, but he keeps telling them to bugger off.

HENRY: I do not. I maintain these jars and we Gassers are one big happy family. So stick out your index finger and descend buttwise on it, Clarissa.

CLARISSA: Well, I think they're disgusting.

GARY: (back in shadows) Hey, there's whole foetuses here.

HENRY: You leave those children alone! Who is this prick, some prick of some slurp conscience, does he think?
(*furious*)
One hand tied behind my back, Clarissa! One hand tied behind my back!

CLARISSA: Henry, you're being ridiculous. If deep down it's just you thinking I'm going to leave with your precious money, don't worry. It's too late.

HENRY: (stopping) I never mentioned any money.

CLARISSA: I did. The bank was very good about your stroke.

HENRY: What stroke?

CLARISSA: The stroke the bank was very understanding about. You might miss a bit of money, Henry, but you'll be comforted to know I'll miss not having it more.

HENRY: Bullshit, Clarissa, and you know it.

CLARISSA: What's all that difficult wriggly stuff underneath your signature anyway? It looks so faked. Even the bank said it looked faked. I just told them of course it looks fake; it always looks fake.

HENRY: It's called a bloody rubric, Clarissa, and it took me years to make it make me look superior. I'll see you both put away!

GARY: (half emerging with a specimen jar) Is that said to me? Is it my turn?

CLARISSA: If you think he'll listen

GARY: Hen, you've got to look at the broader perspective.

HENRY: (slyly) Where do I know that voice from?

GARY: Good old Hen.

HENRY: You're that bodgy Abo rights little turd come to me about my father.

GARY: Sorry, Hen.

HENRY: You let him stay after I booted him out? You're a bloody woman, Clarissa.

(She turns away so as not to answer)

HENRY: Clarissa, he's only using you to get at the jars! Wise up, bloody Clarissa, a post graduate! Post graduates, you can't go lower, Clarissa!

(GARY takes mobile to ring again. She grabs it from him.)

CLARISSA: We said no more mocking.

HENRY: I suppose he's claiming some tinge of some second cousin or something's in one of those jars.

GARY: Naw, they handed my mob extinction long before your old man gave us the shits, Hen.

HENRY: Tasmanian! Jesus H., Clarissa, nobody leaves home for a Tasmanian unless you've got Alzheimers or remember how life has no meaning. What you're doing is the pits, Clarissa.

CLARISSA: (sadly, against them all) You're right, Henry, you should get us booted out.
(*to GARY*)
He's right.

(Wanting to leave now, she tries to thrust GARY's mobile phone onto HENRY, but he is too scared to take it.

GARY snatches it back in anger, tries to substitute HENRY's own phone, but, again, the older man shies from taking it)

GARY: (losing temper) Take it or lose it!

HENRY: (shouting) MURDER! MURDER!

(A long pause, where they each literally turn away 'into' themselves Finally:)

CLARISSA: I read once where it's no good shouting 'murder! murder!' They all do a runner. You have to go 'rape! rape!'. That pulls the crowd.

(Another pause. HENRY has a thought, gropes for receiver of his own phone, listens.)

HENRY: Dead. Very funny, Clarissa.

(She chortles. She moves to GARY and their shadows merge as they slip back into the shadows.)

HENRY: I'm talking to you, Clarissa.

CLARISSA: (speaking 'off' with difficulty) You were not.

HENRY: I was talking to him!

CLARISSA: Who's stopping…
(*sexual climax*)
… yoooooouuu?

HENRY: I'm telling you, Clarissa. He's going to dump you like a four-hour-old prune. Not that I'm saying that definitely. He might prefer a four-hour-old prune and couldn't get past you.

(She re-appears, recovering breath)

CLARISSA: Henry, all I can do is solemnly promise I won't be throwing your money around willy-nilly. It's only my dowry back anyway.

HENRY: You didn't give any dowry.

CLARISSA: Well, now I can next time, can't I?

HENRY: Is that supposed to be funny?

CLARISSA: No, you're right. Gary here mightn't even want the ten thousand you've promised him for my dowry.

HENRY: He'd be lucky.

CLARISSA: I negotiated it on your behalf, Henry.

HENRY: (calls) Cheap at half the price and riddance, Slurp old curry.

CLARISSA: Not ten thousand local. US dollars, Henry.

HENRY: (realisation) Piss off, Clarissa! You take your thieving grubbers off my dollars!

CLARISSA: (sweet logic) Holidays in ashrams in India only look cheap by the brochure, you know. You have to have extras, you know. And, Henry, you'd laugh. I'm going to wear those red spots on my forehead like someone shot me.

HENRY: It's called a pottu, the eye of the God Shiva, you moron. Jesus H., Clarissa, it's your own culture back a bit.

CLARISSA: It still looks like someone has shot you.

HENRY: (maudlin again) You promised you wouldn't leave me alone with my thoughts.

CLARISSA: Don't be such a sook.
(*over shoulder to shadowy GARY*)
I think I'm ready now.

GARY: I'm thinking like maybe we could think of leaving the old fellah alive and stuck with those thoughts he's worried about.

HENRY: (desperate cunning) Absolutely! I haven't got one bit of memory that's not excruciating to live with! You'd know that, Clarissa. So torment me! Leave me alive with them!

GARY: Then again maybe a clean snap's still the better go.

HENRY: Jesus H.... I'm a broken man already! Don't touch the arms! And the legs! You're right! Just leave the breathing bits! He's right, Clarissa! All thinking ever did for the human race was invent no screwing granny! Clarissa, look; I'm shaking thinking with fear here!
(*but gets no response*)
Clarissa?
(*cries out*)
CLARISSA, YOU'LL HATE YOURSELF IN THE MORNING LIKE OTHER PEOPLE DO!

(She re-appears)

CLARISSA: They all say that.
(*then changing mind again*)
Dammit, how can I leave him like this?

GARY: (sternly) Did you make any real promise? Think.

HENRY: Don't think; you'll strain yourself, Clarissa!

CLARISSA: (thinking) It might have been a long time ago...

HENRY: Clarissa, you know you get sick thinking!

CLARISSA: Well, I don't think I promised anything in so many words.

(*cheerfully*)

No, I didn't. God, that's a relief, Henry. I don't even know why I was giving it a second thought really.

HENRY: (into air) Clarissa, forget what I said about thinking! There's not one human thought put on the shelf of the Great Scheme of Things. It's better if we all stick with the idea of God knocking something off the sideboard and it hit the shithouse floor shattering into lots of little pieces. Big, big Bangclatter, see; nothing to disturb your brow's pimples over. Don't think, Clarissa; just think of the Heavenly Misguided Elbow. Clarissa...!

CLARISSA: (now just a voice again) He'll just go on like this for hours if we stay.

GARY: (ditto) Look on the bright side why don't we?

HENRY: Yes, I know that bloody bright side of yours, Slurp, you slippery slope. Like, cancer's just an opportunity of losing weight. Right? And HIV is just AIDS way of cleaning up the world's needle industry. Oh, and who's really dying? It's not death; it's just an event in bloom. Sod you both

(*fearful hiss*)

Clarissa?

CLARISSA: (back again) I gave you plenty of warning, Henry.

HENRY: Wait, wait. Forget the thoughts. I haven't got any thoughts! It's all black in here and blank and I'm frightened out of my wits.

HENRY: Clarissa!

(But she has faded again)

HENRY: (into air) Clarissa, what say we just overlook you trying to think about figuring a few things out! You weren't ever good at it anyway; you did much better without it. Clarissa...?

CLARISSA: (just a voice again) I told you he'd continue for hours like this if we let him.

GARY: And I suggested, as to that, we look on the bright side, Clarry.

HENRY: Clarry? Clarry? Oh, that's very post grad!
(*another fearful hiss*)
Don't do this, Clarissa.

CLARISSA: (back again) I gave you fair warning, Henry.

HENRY: Wait, wait.

(But they speak 'over' him)

GARY: We only taking things that fit in the pocket or the overnight bags?

CLARISSA: Small and expensive, I think. But what do we do about the key? Or leave the front door wide open like someone broke in and… kapow, poor Henry?

HENRY: Oh, God…

(Then sound of a car horn outside)

CLARISSA: (relieved) That'll be Prema with the taxi.

HENRY: PREMA!

(They wait almost with interest to see if anything would result from his shouting. But nothing, except another impatient toot of the horn. They discuss him.)

GARY: Is that fear or a leer he's got on?

CLARISSA: I actually don't know.

HENRY: I'd bloodywell right here, you know.

CLARISSA: If it looks like he's winning at cards, it's a leer. If it looks like he's looking in a mirror, it's more guilt than fear.

HENRY: (into air) I told you I've nothing to be guilty about! I was too young!

CLARISSA: (stopping) Prema didn't tell me you told her that.

HENRY: (miserably) I know I did. It was the confessional box, Clarissa.

CLARISSA: I'm surprised she even came back with the taxi.

HENRY: If I admit it, would we be all right, Clarissa?

CLARISSA: No, Henry.

HENRY: Why not?

CLARISSA: You cheated me.

HENRY: I did not!

CLARISSA: I don't know what you did exactly, but you did it, and I've had my fill of it.

HENRY: Just because I never took you back to Australia.

CLARISSA: Yeah, and you did that deliberately too.

HENRY: I gave up my eyes to keep you out of Australia?

CLARISSA: I wouldn't put anything past you, Henry Gusser.

HENRY: (near fury) Gasser! Jesus H., Clarissa, it's your own name!

(*sheer 'displacement' babble*)

Six years of marital bruises, Slurp old stork, and she can't say her own name right. Is it stupidity? With Clarissa, stupidity would be a fair conclusion, but in this case I think it's more with the subconscious, as in her permanent state of mind and which you should bear in mind. I think it's got to be old Gusser, as in she just has to try to horn in on my metaphor. Gusser as in Old Gus, the carl, Old Gusher. What else? Yeah, ancient old Gussy, gutsache, come a cropper as in gutser. What's she going to call you, Slurp? You may straddle my big toe, Clarissa.

CLARISSA: Nice and charming.

HENRY: Any chance of them stretching your fanny past six feet and calling you Copper? They could market it as a hammock for sailors.

CLARISSA: Really choice.

HENRY: Clarissa, are you sulking with me or siding with him?

(She doesn't answer. Instead, again there is heavy, threatening breathing from the darkness around him. Finally:)

HENRY: All right, get it over with.

CLARISSA: (suddenly after menacing pause) Oh, come on. It's not as though we're leaving you alone, Henry.

HENRY: (hopefully) Prema?

CLARISSA: ('negative') Margaret, one of my first cousins. Least I think this one's called Margaret. You're lucky she was free and has got no standards whatsoever.

(*calls*)

Margaret?

(An answering movement indicates MARGARET has stepped forward.)

HENRY: Not more of your family, Clarissa! There can only be vultures left.

CLARISSA: There's nothing wrong with my family.

HENRY: Nothing that nuclear fall-out wouldn't fix. I'm not here! I've gone fishing!

CLARISSA: It's too late, Henry. She's made up her mind.

HENRY: I'll throw hissy fits! I'll need changing!

(But CLARISSA has faded and MARGARET comes into his sphere.

He will talk as she sidles gradually up to him, tangles herself around him, is inexorable...)

MARGARET: Sir, my man, he beat me. Big big bruises. You look, sir.

(She cocks her leg into his hand)

HENRY: Clarissa! You get back here and get this relative's leg off me!

CLARISSA: (long way off) Goodbye, Henry.

MARGARET: (clawing him for attention) Sir... sir...

(We hear the front door close. The phone rings. He manages to reach it over MARGARET)

VOICE: It's really a fun old day out here under the soothing sea breezes, Henry old man. The Silk Road routes out of Asia are still wide open and flowing beautifully. Even if you don't keep going and stay here, you'll get oodles of postcards. See you, Hen.

(Phone goes dead again)

HENRY:
(*fury*)
Hen? Hen? Bastard, I'll give him 'Hen'…!

(But MARGARET's physical insinuating makes it impossible to do anything other than gradually give in:)

HENRY: Whatever your Margaret name is, kindly get that thigh off me before my wife comes back in...
(*back to 'out there'*)
CLARISSA!
(*listens, struggles, but CLARISSA and GARY have obviously gone*)
Well, stuff you, Clarissa. I have already turned a blind eye to all of this and if you think I'm joking then I mustn't be.
(*to MARGARET*)
Mmm. That's quite sensitive there… no, there...
(*and*)
So, go on, Clarissa. Flit off, you and your Slurp can't-keep-it-down. You think I'm going to miss you? Trying to engage your mind was like parachuting into over Disney Land.
(back to MARGARET)
I think a little higher and in…?...
(*and*)
Clarissa, I needed a penile engorgement science is not capable of. You slack? What's limp like melting plastic, Clarissa? They've got a nerve to call that a body. I call it a wrecking yard. You forget my father left me with body parts here that I was getting stuck with before you were born. I got aboriginal 200-year-old bits'n'pieces with makeovers that'd make your mirror want to defect, bloody Clarissa.
(*back to MARGARET, with muffled difficulty*)

Just a minute, madam, I'm trying to talk to my wife here.
(*and*)
And another thing, Clarissa. You might be world champ of body slurps, but you forget who you're dealing with here. This be Henry Gasser and he wasn't called Nabokov of the South Seas for nix or nought. It's called literature, bloody Clarissa. It is something that uplifts. It's not your sag, Clarissa. Jesus H, in a few years your crutch will need a sling to counter its swing. CLARISSA, I MIGHT'VE BOTTOMED OUT, BUT YOU'RE STILL SUFFERING GRAVITY BURN!
(*then, stopping, shocked*)
Madam, will you kindly get that smelly thing off the back of my hand....?!
(*is slowly brought to mollification*)
Okay.
Okay.
Okay, but...
but
but
but watch out with the fingernails, 'kay?

(Slow fade to end first Act as he perhaps struggles, perhaps joins in)

Act 2

(Full lighting up in contrast to Act 1.

Noticeable is that the room has already been considerably thinned of furniture, and especially of knickknacks, although the many specimen jars and bits of skeleton are left lying around the floor.

This thinning continues throughout the act, as per the directions, through the open thievery of MARGARET and her husband KEKE. No one dares interfere

GARY is sitting on a mattress and sheets on the floor in one of the corners, showing he has been there for some time. His presence seems not to be known by HENRY and he is careful not to give himself away, even though it is he who does much of the proper cleaning up around the older man, rather than the few sloppy attempts from MARGARET.

Now, GARY mainly watches HENRY with very caring intensity, or watches MARGARET very disgustedly.

HENRY elegantly puts a banana peel on the table.

Finally, he speaks to MARGARET as she comes in to fiddle ill-naturedly about him)

HENRY: Fastidious little Maggie. Fastidious is not the go of it. The truth be known the last eye your employer donated to the Sri Lankan National Marble Museum wasn't all that good as a tombola. You possessed a reasonable pinhead and you weren't ever going to get bowled over by it. But, still fastidious like you, that last eye was, little Maggie. Oh, very fastidious. Before it left the blinking fold, I had this chance of a cornea transplant done in India. Fine, I said to that Clarissa harlot of a wife'o'mine, let's wing it to India. But then I learnt most parts there come from baby farms. Jesus H., how're they going to replace any grown man's worst nightmares out of a baby farm, Clarissa?, I said. Should have questioned their credentials then and there, little Maggie-poos. And if you could have worse than that, worse than that was Indian corneas are going to be brown, right?! So I said to this eye guy, 'You wouldn't seriously be thinking of replacing my azure blue with some Ganges muddy brown, would you, old ham-bone?' You wouldn't believe this but the guy only answered, 'I think you are being over fastidious, Mr Gasser?' Me, being fastidious! So you betcha I come back at him, going: 'You think I'm going to walk around outside of India with one blue Azure and one Ganges brown?' I said, and he said, 'Don't you worry, Mr Gasser, if you want we can always throw in a free red rubber ball for a nose too, ha ha.' So you say fug that, and I say fastidious, Maggie mine, or I'm a horse's arse. Neigh neigh.

(*then*)

Hey, look at this dump. Is this a real shithouse or what?

(*laughing at own joke*)

Well, can someone please tell me if this dump is a real shithouse or what? Ha ha. Oh, you have old Henry very jolly today, Mmmmaggie- mmmine.

(still taking no notice of him, MARGARET leaves the room after tapping him – now noticeably over-familiarly -- on the top of the head. It apparently has become a signal of her leaving.

HENRY puts on the radio headphones. He listens for a while, then shouts to upstairs:)

HENRY: CLARISSA!

(*nothing*)

I know you came skulking back last night, Clarissa! Three days, that's a pathetic attempt at doing the big flit, Clarissa. SO COME DOWN AND FACE THE MUSIC, CLARISSA, BEFORE YOU'RE TOO PLUCKED OUT!

(He gives up so quickly it is obvious that this is not the first time he has shouted at/for her recently.

Indeed, he quickly settles back down and begins to nod off in this midmorning light and under the music's influence.

When he is snoring softly and regularly, GARY quickly gets up and moves to stop the radio from falling off the table. He then returns to his corner, where he thinks better of it, and goes back to the couch by HENRY's chair, which has been made up into a bed (for HENRY).

It looks neatly made up, but GARY obviously knows better. He reefs back the top coverlet to reveal the undersheet and pillows all crumpled up. He remakes the bed properly from MARGARET's sloppy effort.

While there, he also takes the opportunity of properly dusting after her

He is nearly finished tidying up after her, when he hears CLARISSA come down the passageway. He hides in the far corner of the living room.

CLARISSA edges into the doorway.

She listens to HENRY's snoring a long time before she can decide that it is real snoring and not pretense. When she has made up her mind, she moves cautiously over to him, where she begins to search both his table and his person for something.

She gets more desperate as she goes on, so that by the time she is rifling through his last pocket, she is being quite rough. He still does not wake up.

Finally, GARY claps with slow irony:)

GARY: Shaking down a sleeping blind man. Bit low, Clarissa.

CLARISSA: (recovering) Bugger, you, where did you go?

GARY: Well, I did want to go to the john like I said, but sort of found myself sitting in the airport bus back here. Time flies.

CLARISSA: Time doesn't fly. You buzzed off.

GARY: My mind was elsewhere.

CLARISSA: Don't think it wasn't my intention of walking out on you before you could walk out on me. Dirt goes before the broom:
(*then tearfully*)
You were never going to get on that plane.

GARY: I started to feel sorry for the old fellah. His father was a great man.

CLARISSA: Aw, that's so sweet.

GARY: Hey, there was the little matter of the traveller's cheques, Clarissa. They weren't even in your name. They've got old Hen's name all over them and there you are at that bank counter breaking the sound barrier.

CLARISSA: I got a little flustered that's all.

GARY: Flustered? The wind socks didn't even dare move.

CLARISSA: Go ahead, make me the villain of the piece. Any decent woman capable of a little scream would do the same when she's trying to give her rotten husband the bullet and finds the rotten sod has beaten her to it. Anyway, what about you, bugger, you? You don't come back here. No one thinks he's got me over any barrel. I do the barrel work here.

GARY: Now, that's a thought.

CLARISSA: You wish. No barrel makes me any old pushover a second time.

(The thought of sex stops their immediate conversation.

They both instinctively check that HENRY is still sleeping.

Then GARY indicates that specimen jars that are now strewn around the floor given that so much of the furniture has been taken)

GARY: This stuff. Even to me, it's weird.

CLARISSA: Don't even talk to me about it.

GARY: Floating around in their own kinda dream time. I've been thinking: what he's got around here, you could like make maybe a whole dude, maybe even a dude-ess, maybe even a leftover kid for them. Slap on some duct tape, and here we go along the old totem trail again.
(*picks up a pelvis bone*)
Me Gorgeous George, and...
(*chases a reluctantly-giggling her*)
you Gorgeous Gorge.

(HENRY suddenly rallies and babbles irrelevantly:)

HENRY: Bits'n'pieces? Actually, you could say Dad's pickle jars are hepped up or herpes'd down, but I say they are all heres-and-theres in the family way. Say otherwise and you would also be overlooking the true symmetry therein. Let me tell you, if you think my Daddy Professor William A. Gasser was all that you saw standing up there ponst his pedestal, it twas not so. I, who attended the back room of the funeral parlor on behalf of myself by sneaking in as a teenager, can attest that these 'ere pickle jars' famous collector and pickler was himself all bits'n'pieces, parts and parcels. You had to be there in that quiet room out back where they were putting him all together again. Humpty Dumpty. Attendez the symmetry! I, with my sneaky eyes, got to see my Pops had two rows of false teeth. Along the bottom jaw, ha ha. More than that, he still had still old glue on the top of his head while they were giving his wig a good hoovering. They were shaving his armpits because it was in his will. Vanity; all was vanity. They were going on about how his left leg was shorter than his right by two inches… and, what's more, the same in centimetres… which I never knew, but they had a set of spare built-ups they would have to remember to put on the bill. Talking of back lighting, I didn't know he had hair entangled in his shoulder blades. Who shaved him after Mum went? They said his Jockeys weren't worth saving. Shitting his pants, one of them asked. No, another undertaker said, just subpar hygiene. Don't you just hate sarcasm from the embalming floor? In death as in life, you can see how my Daddy resembled his pickle jars and his pickle jars resembled him. So I say to all… as a son who was always sneaking around him, can I be fairer than that? And frankly if that confuses you, what I suggest is you roll your head around your eyes, not your eyes around your head. Who said it runs in the family? Now, if some kind soul could send over a morning banana and some some tea, black, half scoop sugar…?

(Just as suddenly, he 'crashes' back to snoring again)

GARY: How does he do that?

CLARISSA: He says it's his Third Eye. He would.

(But HENRY suddenly starts up again:)

HENRY: They had his ears pinned down with Wrigley's bubble gum. Mark that: bubble gum not Spearmint chewy gum. They said that was in his will too.
I've always thought that bubble gum was really important.

(then instantly falls back to snoring again.

They wait for it to happen again, then when it doesn't, they resume:)

GARY: I studied the Professor. The old man as bad as he says?

CLARISSA: (shrugging) There's the son. What do you think?

GARY: To tell the truth, Clarry, I don't know why I came back here. I guess I really did want to see how it panned out for him.

.

CLARISSA: That's really daggy.

GARY: How was I to know crime could be so fascinating?

CLARISSA: Don't you start trying to butter me up.

GARY: (referring to earlier) Okay. So what's supposed to be in his pockets?

CLARISSA: Don't you go all moral on me!

GARY: Sorry.

CLARISSA: (disgusted) Him calling his corrupt mates just to stop a few rotten travellers cheques, how mean can you get? He's always doing that.
(*then at HENRY*)
Corruptor!
(*back to GARY*)
Anyway, it's none of your business, but I was just looking for something that should've come today.

GARY: A brown envelope maybe?

CLARISSA: (over-eagerly) Where?

GARY: I'd guess you're too late.

(He nods out through the door as a hint)

CLARISSA: Margaret, that slut?
(*he shrugs*)
Did it look banky?

(He shrugs 'guess so'. She rushes out of the room, making for the kitchen.

Instead of just standing there, he decides to go to HENRY to continue to make him more comfortable.

Sounds of squealing off, which spills over into the room, as CLARISSA roughs up MARGARET while frisking her. Eventually, she pulls the brown envelope from out of the woman's bra.

She flings MARGARET back towards the kitchen, quickly opens the envelope, extracts cash, and counts.

She is clearly disappointed, oddly smells the envelope with distaste)

CLARISSA: Sss, I should be down at Quarantine committing myself after that woman's been at it.
(*then suspiciously*)
What's she got a bra on for anyway? Last time she wore one family legend has it that even repelled the flea powder they tried to put on it.

GARY: (changing subject) You wearing bra and knickers, Clarry?

CLARISSA: You've got no hope.

GARY: Yes, I do.

CLARISSA: You walked out on the right to ask that, bugger, you.

GARY: Is this lilac time I smell in the air?

CLARISSA: Dream on, lover boy

GARY: (indicating brown envelope) Mucho dinero?

CLARISSA: You're not getting a brass razoo.
(*maudlin*)

How could you leave me standing in the middle of an international airport? Bugger, you. Anyway, I'm out shopping. Do feel free to be gone when I get back.

(She exits angrily, shouting at MARGARET to get up and start working as she goes.

GARY moves over to behind HENRY, puts the slipped earphones back on his head, is in the process of straightening him up, when CLARISSA looks back in)

CLARISSA: Just that do you think you're doing to my husband?

GARY: I'm thinking the volume. Wanna see a nervous system?

CLARISSA: You wake him up midway and he'll come out of it mouth-motoring. I warn you: it'll drive you crazy.

(But before this, she is pushed aside by KEKE, MARGARET's husband, who strides workmanlike into the room.

He is the one who is hoisting the things from the room. This time she and GARY watch while the fellow takes the last painting from the walls. He balances it under one arm so he can get his other arm's fingers into a porcelain vase and then goes out again.

There is no excuse me, or by-your-leave, or furtiveness in his behaviour)

GARY: Mr Joviality Papua New Guinea.

CLARISSA: (but only to get back at him) Don't you start on my family. That man has had to slave like a dog without work to get where he is.

GARY: He's a thief. I've seen him in the street.

CLARISSA: That man has had to thieve his fingers to the bone to get where he is.

GARY: Old Hen said your crowd would swoop in like a plague of locusts.

CLARISSA: If he said that, it was only a lucky guess. That poor struggling man has to overcome being married to that slut of a Margaret out there.

GARY: (realization) Hey, maybe our Clarissa is like getting a bit of her own back...?

CLARISSA: If you think I'm stupid enough to let these termites eat me out of house and home just because they call themselves family, you don't know me beyond what you've known of me biblically.

(This time she does leave properly.

Alarmed by the older man's stentorious breathing, GARY tries to gently wake HENRY. In doing so, he cannot resist in twiddling with the radio's volume control. When he first turns it up carefully, nothing happens. He does it again. Still nothing.

He repeats this until he turns it up and down viciously. It can clearly be heard even through the earphones.

HENRY still doesn't wake up.

Finally, GARY carefully removes the headset.

This slightest touch does wake HENRY up. In one fell movement, one hand drops protectively onto the radio, while the other grabs and keeps hold of, GARY's shirt tail -- and, as though nothing has interrupted him.

He thinks it is MARGARET returned, and naughty-naughty

jiggles the shirt tail)

HENRY: Maggie lickle. Oh, come 'ere come 'ere come 'ere…
(*tries to reel her/GARY in, momentarily gives up*)
'Oh she tried to be a baker's daughter but only came out a tart…' See the poems born lightly and but too brightly, Maggie? Think the lightest of lullabies emerging from the lightness of my touch on your little-less delights so bake-bready, so moonbreaky, so bright light and spritzy. Come ere come 'ere give's a great guzzle you oughty naughty noughty nixsy-vixsy trixie…
(*gives up on the tug-of-war as unwinnable*)
I know I know I know there's me and my Dads in his funeral parlour and you makes three. Deft death touch! Standing with his forefinger in his fob and one hand behind his back, my Poppa was always the photogenic deft touch when not lying down under the undertaker. Who knew, dyou?, that hair piece was made from dingo's hair? I was told from a very knowledgeable source that it was dyed especially to look like real fox fur. Oh, yes, Daddy loved those bits'n'pieces sticking to him! One would never see him digging up tribal graves without meticulously hanging the pieces from the bottom of the braces of his pants. What he did not dangle, he left to the dingoes ha ha. And why? Because my Daddy was a humanist who insisted only the best parts of human beings presented themselves for a dog's proper dinner, that's why. That was no light thing of an insight, Maggie-waggie.
(*mock whine, trying to reel GARY in again*)
Maggie, I am in sweet pain come come come come…
(*into the resulting tug-of-war stalemate:)*
Little minx, you, you just look eye to eyeball at Pop's Pickle Jars there and the poetry of light comes dancing back into rhyming couplets. Somewhere back there is a skull that was as round as a ball. In Dadda's back seat of the old Olds trundling back to Adelaide, that scone of a skull kept rolling around the floor and banging into my little bare feet. It still scares the seven bells of hell out of me, and listen, listen…
(*tries a quick tug, then leaves it again*)
little Meg, should you engender your dainty ring lightly ponst these ring fingers. I promise a heft-it and a hoist-it and a weft-it for its full carat worth. Alternatively, I wouldn't say no-no to a great

draft of some really smelly part of your anatomy, no sirree. Just put it there, pardner.
(*yells*)
CLARISSA? YOU'RE IN THE GUINNESS BOOK OF RECORDS AS A TWO-FISTED JOB!
(*then*)
O. Oo. Little Maggie…

(He makes a successful grab for the other hand; in the resultant new tug-of-way, registers its roughness, and:)

HENRY: Girlie, these dainty mitts shouldn't feel like they've been rubbing down buffalo hides. Try plastic surgery. Find me my brown envelope and I'll even pay.

(He stops when KEKE openly, loudly, comes back into room to look for something else to remove.

This proves this time to be some brass figurines. He noisily departs, a bit disgusted by looking underneath the statuettes and seeing quality that is obviously not to his high expectations.)

HENRY: Doesn't that bugger even take a tea break?
(*shrugs it away anyway*)
Never mind, Mags meggsie, not when it all boils down to how life affect the old angle of the old dangle, my little doxsie.
(*GARY quickly pulls his hand away*)
Margareteski, let's talk filthy foldable kina...
Oh, there was a bell-ringer from Ding-a-Ling
Who bonked a maid out of her Ring-a-Ring...
(*and*)
Willst take a cheque, little Maggie? By the way, you say yes or no to seeing my brown envelope...?

(In his fumbling for it beneath him -- while keeping a hold on her/GARY -- he is unaware that some cheque falls to the floor.

He finally gives up the search)

HENRY: Well, you could always open your mouth, bend down and come in low, ha ha?

(Though still held by the shirt tail, Gary is able to pick up the piece of paper. He examines it while half-heartedly at tug-of-war stretch and, while HENRY carries on, is clearly amazed at what he is holding)

HENRY: (poutingly) Come on, Meggiemag, here's your Henry's white corpuscles baying for infections to fight. Transmit what you will in your familiar strain. Margaret! For pity's sake, I will marry you! Be Mrs Henry Gasser!
(*shouts*)
CLARISSA, IF YOU WEREN'T ALREADY ON YOUR BACK YOU'D BE FEELING THE KNIFE GOING INTO IT!

(GARY extricates himself finally, gives him a triumphant 'bird' with his forefinger, but almost inevitably HENRY by instinct catches his hand and brings it to his lips.)

HENRY: Ah, your pinkie. This delicate thing, overlooking the callouses, carries with it such heavy sweat glands! Thank you, thank you, Maggie dear! I have begun many a ripe old session with pinkies of all sorts, if not ones quite like the texture of sandpaper like this. Never mind, we'll just have to suck it and see, won't we?

(GARY grunts and heaves to get his little finger out of HENRY'S mouth, but HENRY fights to keep it there, and:)

HENRY: Did ooze say sumpththin…?

(GARY finally wrests himself away, moves quickly out of the room.

He returns instantly with MARGARET, shoves her little finger into the old man's mouth)

HENRY: Gurgle, gurgle, goo.

MARGARET: (automatic routine) Sir, big bruise, sir. You look, sir. That man he hit me.

HENRY: (mouth full) 'Irty swine.

MARGARET: Ow and ow, sir.

HENRY: 'Irty beeest.

MARGARET: (giggling) Sir, sir, you wife, no?

(HENRY stops, even he cannot see she is pointing to CLARISSA now in the doorway)

HENRY: That woman's little pinkie is lost to this house.

CLARISSA: (accusatorily) What about my travellers cheques, bugger, you?!

(HENRY quickly puts back on the radio headphones, pretends not to hear, with:)

HENRY: A bit of sush. These spaceships are new-fangled not like the old ones and I'm trying to negotiate a delicate manoeuvre here. Or have I said that?

CLARISSA: (not going away) You're a rotten spoil sport, Henry Gusser! You and your rotten telephone mates making out you're all respectable businessmen.

(He still plays doggo about her being there. MARGARET actually dares to go in competition with CLARISSA by tapping him on the shoulder)

MARGARET: Sir, sir, you look.

CLARISSA: Margaret, piss off!

HENRY: Margaret, Margaret, if you are ever told to fluff off following one of my giving episodes – as, for example, quiet snoring to the world -- it is only customary, you see. You maybe won't understand this, Maggie, but I always needed a bit of ssh after a bit of the old slap-and-tickle, too. They say it is all guilt for what I have done. Bullshit it was guilt. Or if it was guilt, it was never *all* guilt. Sex and its fetid places of boiled whispers and those Richter Scales of unease in the interns of your mind. The bait knife cometh. You see, the thing is…
(*then*)
… I never did return from Mars.

(And returns bluntly to his radio headset to all other exclusion.)

CLARISSA: (down at him) Honestly. That just goes to show how much of a real shit you are, you dirty old man.

GARY: (to his defense) Hey, fair go, Clarry.

CLARISSA: Well, Prema was right.

GARY: (genuinely not knowing what she means) You keep saying that.

CLARISSA: (rounding on him) And you stop sexting me!

GARY: You said the sex was better.

CLARISSA: I meant with you any distance was better, bugger, you.

(She kicks out at him, misses, then kicks out at HENRY, misses, then rounds on an upstaging MARGARET and heaves her away from GARY and shoves her out of the room)

MARGARET: Ow!

CLARISSA: I'll give you bruises you didn't know existed, missy!

MARGARET: (in her face) OW!

CLARISSA: Oh, go show them out to a priest!

(Shoves MARGARET off, rounds on GARY's dishevelment that he's suffered from fighting off both HENRY and MARGARET)

CLARISSA: So, look what the cat dragged in.

(Self-consciously GARY tries to straighten himself and then, by displacement, tries to tidy up his bedding and HENRY's side table.

CLARISSA watches all this disdainfully)

CLARISSA: Did you have to go for an interview for that?

GARY: (now leaning over HENRY) Give it a break, Clarissa.

(HENRY sniffs GARY's armpit)

HENRY: Maggie Maggie, I am offering my accumulation of wealth but we still aren't making progress on the glands, are we, little minx?

(and settles into headset again)

GARY steps back, takes from his own pocket the piece of paper from HENRY's chair. He so pointedly examines it in front of her that, despite herself, CLARISSA wants to know what it is.

They are 'interrupted' by KEKE returning, yet their attentions remain locked on what GARY is holding. They take as much notice of KEKE as the Sri Lankan takes of them... very cursory. But they are mindful enough of him not to move, and only discreetly half-watch, while he continues looting the room.

KEKE is down to having to take the drapes off the windows. These he takes by simply ripping them off, opening the windows and throwing them outside and looking out through the window bars to see if they have landed within his later reach.

Not much is left in of the furniture now. He takes a screwdriver out of his sarong and begins to unscrew the brass door fittings. But he decides he needs a new screwdriver and will go out to fetch one. Meantime...)

CLARISSA: (gives in re GARY's piece of paper) All right, I'll bite.

GARY: (deliberately suggestive) Don't you ever.

CLARISSA: Just tell me what it is.

GARY: I think you'll find it mildly amusing.

CLARISSA: Something you might have? I don't think so.

GARY: It's not me having it. It's old Hen's giving it.

CLARISSA: (trying to snatch it) That's mine!

GARY: How do you know?

CLARISSA: If he's giving anything, it's mine by what's-coming! Hands off.

GARY: (toying with her) He hasn't actually given it.

CLARISSA: (suddenly fed-up) Who cares? He's just an old pervert.

HENRY: (sudden descry, into air) I AM NOT!

CLARISSA: Oh, sure, he's all pins-and-needles when it's all about him.

(She goes over and claps her hands loudly by his ear. HENRY doesn't react. She claps her hands suddenly and threateningly in his face. He doesn't see nor hear this. She lifts one earphone – we hear the radio – and HENRY instantly cringes.

She lets the earpiece fall back on his ear, and he calms down immediately, settles back into contentedness)

CLARISSA: See? It's all him. How perverted can you get?

GARY: You just won't let up, will you?

CLARISSA: You wouldn't even want to know what Prema heard.

GARY: Yes, I would.

CLARISSA: These lips are silent.

GARY: No, they're not.

CLARISSA: These lips are sealed.

GARY: No, they're not.

CLARISSA: (perversely back at HENRY) PERV!

HENRY: (dully into air) I am not. It's the bait knife. Shove it right in, they said. All I did was do what they said.

CLARISSA: (more forcibly) You diddled dirty, didn't you, pervert?

(Now she tears the headphones right off him, holds them out of reach)

CLARISSA: Diddler!

HENRY: (in reverie, indirect) Who said under-age? Oh, they were the sizzler's sons and the salivable daughters but the sausage got their savvies…

CLARISSA: Diddler!

HENRY: (miserably) No, please.

GARY: All right, Clarry.

HENRY: (to GARY's direction) I know you're here, too. Slurp the dork. Have you come to finish it, Slurp? Don't hurt me. It doesn't tickle.
(*then*)
It's all a mistake, you know. I tried to tell Prema there are metaphors that sharply come out of the deep…

CLARISSA: (interjecting) Oh, she got it. How would you feel if indecency drove you out of here and back home into the arms of having to look after her eight kids?

HENRY: (deadened) But she didn't understand But a confession. But not like that. But I think I spoke of tooth, hair, skin, flippers fishing. But I know I told her about the sharp point and the slithering edge and open mouths unto the blade.

CLARISSA: Rubbish and you know it!

HENRY: (now reduced to nodding) At the last few inches, you feel how it oozes in and oozes out. They called it a bait knife, you know. Listen, Clarissa, I admit in my mind they are guilts but they have no name and... and besides they taste like strawberry and I can't resist strawberry, how it cuts.

(*then, agony, shouting upstairs*)

CLARISSA, I NEVER LEARNT TO TELL THE SPATE OF HEAVEN FROM THE SPATE OF HELL!

CLARISSA: Rubbish, all rubbish!

(With disgust she puts the earphones roughly back on his head, turns away.

This is in timing with KEKE returning with a new screwdriver, with which he proceeds to remove the brass door parts.

He goes about this silently while the others carry on as though he isn't even there. It is only when he gets into strife with removing the hinges and holding up the door that his struggles disrupts them. Meanwhile, though...

...GARY has taken pity on the old man following CLARISSA's verbal assault. He carefully places the earphones back on HENRY's head. The old man nods gratefully, can 'sink' back into listening.

GARY steers CLARISSA out of the old man's earshot. They don't even glance at KEKE)

GARY: How about calling a truce on it, Clarry.

CLARISSA: Call yourself a dead shit. No, call the cops. No, I will.

(She stares him down, pulls away and defiantly helps KEKE with the door hinges.

When he has them, he doesn't thank her, merely takes the door from her, leaves it leaning against the door frame, then pushes her out of the way as he leaves with the brass fittings.

HENRY starts snoring.

KEKE returns for the door itself. He heaves it away from the wall, stands with it, looking expectantly at CLARISSA. She points to GARY but KEKE shakes his head so commandingly that she herself obediently moves to help her brother-in-law to carry the door out)

CLARISSA: (covering up humiliation) I've always wanted this.

GARY: It's already yours.

CLARISSA: That's not the same

(They exit, KEKE kicking at least one specimen jar contemptuously out of the way so that the door can be manoeuvred out and down the passageway.)

GARY: (re the jars) Careful!
(*then down the passageway after her*)
Your mob live in tents, Clarissa?

(He knows to wait.

Soon, she returns dusting off her hands as a job well done)

CLARISSA: So what if they do live in tents, smart bugger, you.
(*then*)
You know, I never slapped men.

GARY: Aw.

CLARISSA: I just kick them in the cods instead.

GARY: Whoa...

CLARISSA: And don't think I don't know what you're on about, sneaking back in here. I bet you did catch the bus back.

GARY: (shrug, self-consciously) Bit light on for a cab.

CLARISSA: First thing, we don't let people who have to catch buses into this house, let alone back in.

GARY: (waving the piece of paper again) But look how useful I am.

CLARISSA: (deliberately obtuse) You have come back to harm and extort my husband, you just happen to run into the second thing. This second thing is we do not let people who're out to do us harm into this house.

GARY: My ears burning or didn't you suggest it?

CLARISSA: I was just quirking. We like to quirk. It runs in my family. Quirk, quirk. Bugger, you.

GARY: (could be real menace) We were talking how, not if.

(She pulls herself up on the thought that he might mean it and, if he does, then it could involve both her and HENRY now.)

CLARISSA: Hey. Don't go going mad.

(She edges towards the door. Now enjoying himself, he moves to place himself smirkingly between her and it.)

GARY: We weren't talking quirks.

CLARISSA: (placating) Think quirks. I don't mind.

GARY: I don't like quirks. Irks, irks.

(He holds the menace for a long moment, then breaks it

with a laugh and moves away.)

GARY: (mockingly) Aw, and I thought we were partners in crime.

CLARISSA: (outrage) That was only in the face of overwhelming climaxes.

GARY: Good climaxes, Clarry.

CLARISSA: Oh, stop it. You worry about the climax of my family removing you like they did that door... stiff as a board.

GARY: That's not bad, Clarry.

CLARISSA: It's as fake as the climaxes. Call me the faker and you the fakee.

(He is now pendulum-ing the piece of paper in front of her)

CLARISSA: Not with this, no fakee, Clarry.

(He continues dangle it before her until she falls for the tease again and tries to snatch it, but misses)

GARY: Here's a hint. It was sort of fixed to your brown envelope.

CLARISSA: Oh yeah? What's that, the address label?

GARY: Probably better than money, I reckon.

(This makes her stop and think.)

CLARISSA: I said, that's mine!

(He allows her to read it at a distance, but keeps his finger over one side of it)

GARY: (reciting) 'Pay Mrs Clarissa E. L. J. Gasser' the sum of...

CLARISSA: (greedily) Get your thumb out of the way!

GARY: Guess.

CLARISSA: You might tear it! Be careful!

GARY: (quite seriously) Ywanna fight me for it? I mean a real go?

CLARISSA: (stopping) Don't start getting het up again.

(But all this is temporarily stalled while KEKE returns, shimmies open a sideboard door he has sussed out before as being locked, disgustedly takes out a couple of specimen jars and shoves down on the floor as useless, removes valuable knick-knacks, departs sourly.)

GARY: (again) Come on, Clarry. Guess.
(*she gives him the bird*)
Would you believe a thousand? Ten thousand?

CLARISSA: (interest lost) I'd believe ten fullstops less change, that's what I'd believe. Use it for your bus fare out of here. No, don't bother. By the time the next bus comes along he'll have cancelled it.

GARY: See, that's the beauty... this one can't be canceled. This is a bank cheque. What's more, think one hundred thousand. With dollar signs.

CLARISSA: (shock disbelief) He's joking!

GARY: It's there for you to cash, dumdum. Anywhere, anytime, in the whole wide world. Done deal, no cancelling.

CLARISSA: Bugger, you!

(She rushes at him and, to his amusement, forces him to hand it over.

When she reads the amount, she is amazed)

GARY: (chuckles) Old Hen. What a guy.

CLARISSA: One hundred thousand dollars.

(GARY moves back over to HENRY and ruffles his hair. The old man cringes, but stays 'within' the safety circle of his radio, though his eyes stay wildly open.)

GARY: (chuckling over him) You old fraud.

(He turns back to her. She is too busy inspecting the cheque against the light for some catch to it all)

GARY: That'd just about clean the old fellah out, wouldn't it?

CLARISSA: (distracted) Could do.

GARY: It'd make you stop to think how much it shows he thinks of you, wouldn't it?

CLARISSA: Might do.

GARY: You'd have to be thinking hey, is this the height of violins and moonlight or what, wouldn't you?

CLARISSA: Probably.
(then 'returning')
Are you saying something I could possibly want to listen to?

GARY: You'd have to be thinking hell the old fellah's just a big old romantic at heart, right?

CLARISSA: Not even if he was standing in the middle of a heart attack.

GARY: (actually quite earnest) No, see, it's actually what I think I came back for… to see how far it'd all go.

(He goes over to HENRY, touches his eyes. HENRY cringes, but GARY calms him, literally closes the old man's eyes as if he was a corpse.

HENRY allows this, sits eyes closed 'within' earphones still)

GARY: This being an old softie can get to really hurt, can't it?

CLARISSA: Rubbish. He's only doing it to make me feel bad.
(*pause before cheque wave*)
I just got better.

GARY: Remember me? I'm the bearer of good news.

CLARISSA: Like you said, you walked out on me. I didn't walk out on you.

GARY: You did. You said you were going to at the first opportunity. You got seats on separate rows on the plane.

CLARISSA: I was just trying to make myself feel better.
(*brief cheque wave*)
I got better.

GARY: You think I'm going to let you get away with that?

CLARISSA: I do. Now that I can afford to say 'I do'.

GARY: You think?

CLARISSA: I do. See there it is already. It means don't mess around with money and the friends it can buy.

GARY: (amused) Okay, Clarry, what's next?

CLARISSA: What's next is I'm going to thank God.

GARY: Seriously.

CLARISSA: I'm going to thank God seriously.

GARY: Really seriously.

CLARISSA: I'm going to really seriously thank God He made my loving husband think of it. Then I'm going to use it really seriously like my loving husband intended, as in spending really seriously big, bugger, you. Did you notice I only used 'I' there and not any royal 'we'?

GARY: Finder's fee, Clarissa.

CLARISSA: This good and generous man there puts you to shame Oh, look, does this read 'Pay Mrs Clarissa E. L. J. Gasser' and not mention you? Oo, did the wind just change? Is my smirk fixed on my face?

GARY: All right, now I'm kicking myself. That make you happy?

CLARISSA: Oh, don't kick yourself. It might hurt. Shoot yourself instead.

> *(This happens to coincide with KEKE having just come back in and proceeding to unscrew one of the davenport's lead-glass doors.*
>
> *She goes over to him and taps him on the shoulder. When he straightens she points to GARY)*

CLARISSA: Dispela rausim stret nau!
(*to GARY*)
Hey, student of human nature, that means give you the boot.

(But KEKE isn't moving to do that. Instead he is taking stock of them both.

CLARISSA remembers she is holding the bank cheque openly, pushes it down her bra.

She is not quick enough. KEKE sees what she is doing. He hardly breaks stride in moving to her and pulls her hand away from her bra.

When she refuses to give him the draft, he simply and brutally slaps her across the face. She staggers.

When GARY moves to intervene, KEKE pulls out a fish-gutting knife and threatens him with it a very practiced way.

GARY stops.

KEKE roughly pulls CLARISSA to him, looks at her smilingly for a long time, then simply removes the cheque from her bra. He openly fondles her as he does so – and the way she dares not move shows the real power structure in the family.

Amused, KEKE turns his back on GARY, knowing now he will get no challenge. He then leisurely examines the piece of paper in his hand; it is obvious he knows full well what it is.

Satisfied he turns back, seizes CLARISSA and, with his knife, holds her as hostage)

KEKE: Yupela kona sindaun!

(GARY hasn't a clue as to what was said)

CLARISSA: He says stay in the corner. Do it. He cuts palm cats up with that thing.

(GARY unhesitatingly does so.

In this waiting time, KEKE 'carts' his hostage around the room roughly by the arm while he assesses other things – very few now – he might want. He bends her with him to inspect many of the jars, but even he shows distaste.

Eventually. HENRY takes off his earphones and continues speaking as though he hasn't ever paused...)

HENRY: 'Nearer My God to Thee'?
(*starts heavenward conversation*)
Jesus H., God old Gob, holy-moly on all of us if even you have to use the BBC to get through. A bit hard on Clarissa, was I? Sorry, sorry, but to be honest, old plum duff, those who wouldn't know shit from sugar sometimes might call me Gutsache. One thing, though, old juice... are you going to use the furphy that you reached down and touched me? Could you do me a favour next time and not reach down and touch me? Like, even your oppo Old Nick wouldn't even say he bothered to reach down and touch me, do me down, sort of thing much, right? I mean, his rat fleas no me plagued, 'kay? Malaria, dengue fever, TB, asthma… never sent on their fiery way up to squeeze my nuts in any smithy's vice. There came no honourable sores on the honourable penis. I've been sweating here for ten years Old Nick didn't even posted me the old pricky heat. I mean, he's been a real gent by comparison. Okay, okay, a few itches, qualm-wise, but I've already covered them, quite delicious in their way, and the way he makes it nice to be naughty, it's nice to be naughty. So, yes, Gob of mine, I get all that, but…
(*growing anxiety = bluster*)
your reaching down and touching... I can only say the only good it did me was I never missed perving on any of your ladies' wondrous dancing nates anywhere I went, anytime, ever…
(*a new bout of fear*)
I just don't want you to go leaving me with the wrong idea! All right? All right?...

(As he struggles with himself, CLARISSA starts to rebel

about being hoisted around the room like a rag doll)

GARY: (meaning KEKE) Jesus, Clarry. What's he going to do?

CLARISSA: (plainly fed up) If he doesn't let go of me, he's going to get one right in the goolies.

GARY: Take it easy, Clarry!

(She pushes KEKE off her. He threatens to go at her, then at GARY. They back off.

Instead, anyway, KEKE decides it's more fruitful to move to HENRY and to hold the knife at his throat.

He is far enough away that, at first, HENRY doesn't realise what is going on, but it is close enough for KEKE to be near enough to strike)

CLARISSA: (shouts) MARGARET...?

HENRY: (sniffing a presence) Maggie, Maggie, thou'st keep forgetting the deodorant. Phew and phew I say. Take all the housekeeping money; go to anywhere Pine Fresh is on the shelves and but the whole stock. Try to keep away from them fish markets.

(*then back with God*)

Sorry, God good gorbie, what were we saying?. The thing is, old custard, that touch see and lights-out... I mean, twas my light, old bangers-and-mash. I canst make light of it nor, now, light work. See how your imagery can survive even your attention on any good day? Your poesy should purge, after all. Many pieces immortalized upon the bog roll and before applied to bot, e.g.:
'I looked upon seeing the light-gravure/
The altar candles were lights-out but callow lit the lit-erature.'
Perhaps needs a touch working on by someone cheeky enough to try. But then, don't think I don't get it that we get the pull-through, but not the see-through, right? But, see, old corn on the Gob, I can see all that but what's all the hurry? Give me one

human illumination you've put up on the shelf of the Great Scheme of Things like little Maggie's Pine Fresh? What's wrong with just us staying safe at home happy in the idea that you just knocked something the cosmic sideboard and oops, sorry, crash-tinkle big big Bang there, clumsy old you? I've already put this on the table, you know. What's wrong with you admitting I am right and it was all just being a case of Misguided Elbow?
(*listens*)
Oh, I should consider the value-adds? What're they? Like, the pain you've lumbered us with was just meant to be used recreationally? And love was supposed to come with us paying you royalties? And what are these bodies that need cranking up? Where were we supposed to buy the cranks? You forget about supplying enough cranks? And… and it's not really dying. It's just our local fire-exit plan…? Oh, right, and there was only one Word because grief and strife dead-heated for first…? And, shissake, who'd you leave in charge of the Grand Design? Blind Freddie? Okay, okay, I sort of get all that, old mango, old nanna, old gobful, but, mostly, what's the big mystery? Why's the why? I mightn't be able to touch up my Clarissa anymore, but I've never knocked back copping a feel of a good secondhand car. You see what I'm getting at here? We're made in your image of gobfuls, but what's with you leaving out the right word all the time? For all I know you could have me under the hammer right now...

(He moves a bit sharply for KEKE, who by now has little patience left. GARY quickly cautions)

GARY: Keep it still, Henry.

HENRY: I don't like what in that voice. I don't like what's in his voice, Clarissa!

CLARISSA: For shit's sake, Henry, for once listen!
(*calls out again*)
MARGARET...!!!

(Her tone gets through to HENRY and he stiffens with fright.

But he can just bring himself to reach out very gingerly to feel the knife 'over' him. He runs his hand over its shape, then his fingers along its blade edge.

He nods terribly tiredly, as though what he has always feared has come at last:)

HENRY: (fatally) Yes. 'Kay. Okay, Slurp.

GARY: Just keep still.

HENRY: (very weakly) I just wish it wasn't this guy and I don't know why I say that.

(MARGARET answers the calls and expertly sized up the situation.

As if to demonstrate his meaning more for her, KEKE moves right in on HENRY with his knife and leaves little room for error. He adds surprisingly good English to this manoeuvre:)

KEKE: (to CLARISSA) You bank now. One hour no more, go.
(*at GARY*)
You too, cunt.

(MARGARET walks over to him with her hand out. He only lets her look at the bank cheque, and commands her too:)

KEKE: You bank too. Go!

(He goes to push her off, but she is too quick for him. She feints with one hand and then with the other grabs the cheque out of his hand and, also shoving it down her bra, makes a run for it.

The others double-take at her effrontery.

In rapid succession)

KEKE: Uh!

(and takes off after her)

CLARISSA: Hey!

(and takes off after her)

GARY: Whoa!

(and takes off after her.

HENRY is left alone.

He waits a while before speed dialing, waits as the call goes through with the phone on speakers…)

TELEPHONIST VOICE: Jaya Bank, good morning.

HENRY: The Chairman, ta.

TELEPHONIST VOICE: Who's to speak, please?

HENRY: Tell him Henry.

TELEPHONIST VOICE: Jaya Bank has no Chairman by that name, sorry. Have you tried pressing three?

HENRY: I know Jaya Bank has no Mr Henry!

TELEPHONIST VOICE: Please press two or one if you want a customer rep…

HENRY: Jesus H. Let me talk to Mr Perera.

TELEPHONIST VOICE: Sorry, sir, he isn't in.

HENRY: Bullshit.

TELEPHONIST VOICE: Putting you through, sir.

(The sounds of redirections. Then:)

PEDRO'S VOICE: Henry, good morning. What did I want to talk to you about?

HENRY: I'm ringing you.

PEDRO: She said it was me wanting to speak to me.

HENRY: Well, it's not.

PEDRO: Are you sure?

HENRY: I am.

PEDRO: Are you sure you've discussed it with her?

HENRY: (long suffering) Pedro, how long did you say before the ink fades?

PEDRO: Oh, the draft. Shouldn't be too long now, ha ha.

HENRY: Say, if it's out of its envelope and on a naked run poked down a hot and steamy place only as high or wide as a C cup, and that hot and steamy C cup is bouncing up and down in the tropical midday sun for all it's worth and getting hotter and steamier as we speak…?

PEDRO: Lucky it. How hot and steamy?

HENRY: Please get your mind off that, Pedro. Let's just say very hot and steamy.

PEDRO: If it hasn't already faded, it's sure to go pop imminently, Henry. I would, wouldn't you?

HENRY: Mucho gracioso, Pedro.

PEDRO: No problem, Henry. Now what did I have to talk to you about?

HENRY: Forget it, Pedro.

PEDRO: Hey, Henry, what's our motto?

HENRY and PEDRO: (singsong together) 'Cuckolds of the world's banks unite.'

(cuts off call, then muses for a moment before:).

HENRY: CLARISSA, THE WALLS OF YOUR CUNNY HAVE METAL FATIGUE!

(He uses speed dialing button and succeeds in getting international exchange assistance)

OPERATOR: (without waiting) She doesn't want to speak to you.

HENRY: I haven't said who I wanted yet!

OPERATOR: You don't have to.

HENRY: Yes, I do!

OPERATOR: We are not all mind readers, you know. Please state number, surname, initials, town, region and country.

HENRY: Gasser. I want Dee, Doctor. University of Edinburgh. Scotland. Collect. Tell her it's her father.

OPERATOR: Please hold, Mr Gosher.

HENRY: Gasser!

(but has to wait)

OPERATOR: (heard talking:) Good evening. There is a collect call from the ends of the earth sounding like Pap-all-over. It is from a Mr Henry Grisser or Groper? It's hard to tell. Will you accept the call?

(*apparently listens*)

There's no need to go all beastly, madam. I don't even know the person. I don't even know if you could say a person.

(*might have been hung up on; back to HENRY*)

What a stuck-up bitch! Someone should tell her words would be nice not snortings. Next time you ring up please chose a different name. We shouldn't have to suffer in our professional capacities because of it.

HENRY: Shissake, what did she say?!

OPERATOR: I just said it was a snort, Mr Gropper, which we are not accustomed to here.

HENRY: She's my longlost little girl! Look, young man....

OPERATOR: Woman, thank you so much, as if you'd know.

HENRY: (rising hysterics) You available? No, I didn't mean that. Don't answer that. I'm hopeless. I am an old man alone. I only want to talk to my only daughter, who I have never seen in the flesh at any age where you could call flesh flesh, and now I'm in danger of never-will because I can't see a frog from a fog anymore. They call it being handicapped. I call it as blind as a fucking bat. Oh, God.

OPERATOR: I will make an exception, remembering I am not put here on earth to do so, so I shouldn't, so I will. Here is the message: There is no message as I made abundantly clear. There is snorting on the line which my experience tells me you're in the boghouse. All I can do is ask whether you are willing to accept a snort and I am willing to snort it through.

HENRY: (quickly) I accept!

OPERATOR: (singsong) Putting you through, Mr Guzzler.

HENRY: Gasser!

OPERATOR: (fading fast) I insist on putting you through regardless of you refusing to identify who you really are.

HENRY: (shouts at phone) Dee?

(*sails on regardless, rising nerves*)

Diana, it's Dad! Is that my little daughter breathing? A breath of you is a breath of life to some satellite, ha ha. Not ridiculing; just on the bait knife edge. Never been too sharp as bait and being on Mars never helps. What I wondered: have we just had another anniversary of not having spoken to each other? How many anniversaries does that add up to? Forty, forty-five? Tiny infant you with that hole in the heart, and me born with a big hole in my commitment. See how early on we were tagged for a two-way bypass? But I won't keep you in suspense. Here's the word: it is inheritance. I did; I said inheritance.

(*listens*)

I take that rustle as the sound of ears-pricking-up. Regrettably, I have nothing to give but you know of course I'm talking of your granddaddy's stuff, all his famous pickle jars of tribal bits'n'pieces. They'd still be pawnable if you find the pawn shop I never did no matter how hard I tried. But then you could give Bits'n'Pieces back, fame and fortune will await you back here in the Antipodes. Plaques in your name under exhibition cases. But a fig for inheritance! I wanted to tell you how I loved your mother! Leaving her with a 'see-you-later-Alligator' was really off, I agree. It came out wrongly. Tell her she couldn't have lived with my sulkiness, anyway. I believe Vladimir Nabokov had the same weakness Not that you can compare your mother's stalag to his Stalin, ha ha. Incidentally, I've gone totally blind since we last had the little chat we never had. But then, what's sight but yesterday's tears, ha ha? Tell your mother, will you? She deserves a bit of a giggle after all I did to her. And tell her she was right, I did end up adrift of any finishing line.

(*then*)

Hello? Dee?

(*then*)

Just to see your face. Just to run my fingertips across your cheek. Just to see you against a dawn's slow brightening in rose. Just to have your little breath gentle against my cheek. Girlie! You are still my little girl.

(gathers himself again)

Did I tell you how I donated my last eye to the developing-world's marble stocks? It was my one'n'only bluey too. Well, when I say donated, I mean I said keep the bloody thing if you ever fish it out of the drain you bloodywell dropped it down. They said oops, butter fingers. I said easy-come-easy-go yourselves, you rotten shits. I said, when you airmail my last good cat's-eye back to me, I might consider returning my Pop's parts to you. Hey, I've got a sum part somewhere out there needing a decent burial, too.

(*then*)

So, little girlie, here's the word again. Inheritance. Inheritance, thy name is pickle jars! You will love returning them. Just be careful about what a bloody great kleptomaniac of a grave-robbing maniac they start trying to unearth your famous granddaddy as actually being. Remember, he is blood. He's the old razor I'm attached to! I am the nicked, he the nicker. You ask why should I care when all my life he'd just snorted like a hog whenever he deigned to look at me, saying I was one of history's oddities up-earthed from his own backyard? I've often thought about him and me coming together… do you think glandular secretions might actually be the glue of the universe? I wouldn't know about that, but what I'm trying to tell you here is family is all. No guarantee of reputation, no pickle jars. No eye, no pickle jars. It's family. Until then, they can all go root my boot.

(*pause*)

…Dee? Ah, my little girlie, if there was one thing out of the millions of words I ever tried penning, there's one passage that sticks with me as being worth all the swim. It was written for you my darling my Juliet my Brenda my Caz my Sandy my Sophie my Angela my Mary my Elizabeth my other Sandra my Tessie… and

there has just got to be an Ann in there somewhere. Only for you, though, in a mainly sort of way. Honestly. It was my ululation to you. Listen:
'…Oh, why trellise twilights whilst the trust whimsies true…'
Jesus H., I can't remember anymore! Excusee. I never did invite you up to Mars, did I!? Ssh, ssh, don't cry. Dee, I just think I'm really hurting now. I think this growth I'm told is behind my eye might've slipped its shackles. Dee! I just rang to tell you… I think I'm ready to give you your pickle jars now. Did I say 'your'? I did, I did. See, little girl, they always have been. Your grandpops, it's in his will they're yours. Everything, he wrote, is yours. Even though he had never laid eyes on you, he still preferred you over me. My name wasn't even mentioned in his will. Yet they were handed on to me to pass onto you when the time came. I am caretaker. I am flyblown. I have these jars of pickled stuff on my hands and they weren't intended to be on my hands and I don't want them on my hands but *I can't let them go!*
(*he quietens somewhat*)
And, see, that's the thing, see. It wasn't that I was jealous of you or anything. Never! It's just that I always felt my going blind was my due as the reflection of being unseen between him and you. And, see… see?...
(*can just get out*)
how could you ever love someone so unseen.

(On this he has to stop, sits back wearily.

The connection is broken.

There is a long endgame pause. But then he hears the sound of the others clambering back through the front gate and into the house.

Quickly, he speed dials again)

HENRY: Pedro!

PEDRO'S VOICE: Henry!

HENRY: Congratulations! About the magic ink, hot and steamy's came in first, I think.

TOGETHER: 'Cuckolds of the world's banks unite!'

(HENRY hangs up again. Waits smugly.

It is GARY who returns hot and bothered first. Nevertheless, he notices how HENRY is dishevelled and moves instinctively to tidy him up... even lets HENRY hold his hand.

Now it is HENRY's joke to overtly confuse him with MARGARET)

HENRY: Fussing, little Maggie pie, always on the fuss. Don't you worry; we can certainly sit down and discuss a table of rates re bruises when things settle down...

(gives in a back-of-hand kiss and gets a pat on the shoulder of acknowledgment from GARY, who then makes way for...

CLARISSA staggers back, stares daggers at HENRY, tears up the now-blank bank cheque and throws the pieces at him)

CLARISSA: There's something very wrong with you, Henry Gusser.

HENRY: Gasser, you goat!

(She is shoved aside by KEKE with MARGARET. In rage he moves to HENRY's side table, sweeps all the things off it and goes to take the table itself.

MARGARET rushes to stop him.

They struggle. KEKE gets in a vicious backhand across her chest. But she falls back only momentarily, feints and, very professionally, kicks him in the groin. He is dropped and gladly stays there, defeated.

MARGARET gets back to 'business', pulls out her breast, fronts HENRY)

MARGARET: Sir, that man he beat me. Big big bruise booby…

HENRY: (a bit too weary) Ah, Maggie, ere not too long ago this lap of mine could have greeted that like a happy dog's tail, now what to do?

(So she turns to GARY, shows breast to him)

MARGARET: Sir, that man beat me. Big big bruise.

(He waves her off. She turns to CLARISSA, gets a warning brush-off.

Rejected, she sits in her own space, as others have)

HENRY: Without putting too fine a point on it, I take it all our little inks have now faded in our hot-and-steamies?
(*gets no response*)
Ah well, they say each day was sent to try us. And that's just the sort of jury selection I've always objected to.

GARY: (urges CLARISSA onto him) Use the under-age thing now, Clarry.

CLARISSA: (but only half-heartedly) Pervert!

HENRY (not at all fazed) Ah, the unnamed guilts again. You know I don't know how I ever got along without that bait knife Prema conjured up.

GARY: You can't let him escape so easily as that, Clarry. I'M GOING TO START SHOUTING AT YOU TOO!

CLARISSA: Join the club.

(There is an impasse, until:)

GARY: What about that Prema?

CLARISSA: What about her?

GARY: What she said he told her!

CLARISSA: Good God, mention bait knife or some nonsense like that to that dippy and she'll start screaming you murdered the Pope. She lays on her back to pray.

HENRY: Thank you for that, Clarissa.

CLARISSA: I was the only one you could ever thank, Henry.

HENRY: It's always been a pickle, I know.

(Suddenly a rock shatters the window and then shouting from a mob outside.

All hell breaks loose -- rocks on the roof, other windows being smashed, clubs bashing against walls etc. One of the collection jars is smashed with a rock

They scramble to sit huddled around HENRY's chair for protection but it doesn't take long for KEKE to panic first. He makes a break for it, dashes out)

GARY: (real fear) Can he talk to them?

CLARISSA: ('that's a joke') He's what they're here for. They're the local, he's not. They do the looting around here, not him coming in here and cutting them out.

MARGARET: (throat-cutting motions, happily) Krrrkkkk. Big bruises that man's neck. So long, Buster.

(What sounds like a small bomb goes off very nearby)

HENRY: They're always willing to a small slight into an unholy riot. Always admired that about the Papuans. Shows real tear-away.
(*then, with mounting noise outside*)
Maybe a bit different just now, it obviously having become about us.

CLARISSA: They'll be blaming us for letting our things get into the hands of a thief trying to rob them.

(With a strange and gentle fatherliness, HENRY gently 'gathers' them around him. Strangely, too, they are gladly drawn to him.

The rioting has really grown now and is really at their door)

HENRY: Kiddies mine, it's all right. The thing is to stay tight knit, isn't it? Isn't it?
(*he feels the nods they give*)
We could almost say family, couldn't we?

(CLARISSA looks from GARY to MARGARET and has to admit:)

CLARISSA: We could, Henry.

(As the chaos draws nearer, they huddle around his seat closer)

HENRY: Clarissa, I composed a lullaby for you. It came to me exclusively for you in a most almost way. See if you dare to suggest any changes:
(*in lilt*)
'…Oh, how could you ever love someone so obscene…'

Obscene? Unclean? Jesus H., I still can't remember it! Memory's always a bit of a problem living on a dusty red planet far away, don't you know. Coming back to things, a bit of a problem. BUT YOU SEE I WAS NEVER HIGH ON THE HOG OF INTELLIGENCE, CLARISSA!

(She tugs his trouser cuff)

CLARISSA: I'm just down here, Henry. No need to shout.

HENRY: ('well then':) So do we all have our eyes closed? Maggie?
(*she has; she has her head in his lap*)
Clarissa?

CLARISSA: Yes, Henry.

HENRY: Slurp?

GARY: Yes, Henry.

HENRY: Well, let's hold hands and go back to Mars, shall we?

(The lighting fades until only the central spot on HENRY's 'area' and the group is left huddling against the oncoming rage outside. There are sounds of glass breaking and doors being forced.

Slow fade)

(End)

www.ingramcontent.com/pod-product-compliance
Lightning Source LLC
LaVergne TN
LVHW051703080426
835511LV00017B/2703
* 9 7 8 0 9 9 4 6 3 0 1 0 0 *